Letting Her Go

By Soumaya Cisse

Letting Her Go

بسم الله الرحمن الرحيم

Allah is the Light of the heavens and earth. His
Light is like this: there is a niche and in it a lamp.
The lamp inside a glass. A glass like a glittering
star fueled from a blessed olive tree from
neither East nor West. Whose oil almost gives
light, even when no fire touches it
– Light Upon Light –
Allah guides whomever He wills to His Light.
Allah draws such comparisons for people; Allah
has full knowledge of everything. Shining out of
homes, Allah knew that they would be raised
high and His name be remembered in them.
With people inside swimming in praise of Him
morning and evening.

Quran 24:35-36

Contents

Author's preface

Upon deciding to enter this venture, I hadn't realised what the journey ahead would encompass. Allah had already planned something. And I didn't know it would be filled with so much.

I began my writings in London. My home city and a place with a hidden spiritual hold. Open to those who seek. After the death of my maternal grandmother, I flew to her native village in the Atlas Mountains of Algeria, Kabylia, a place I hadn't been since I was a child. I felt Allah had opened His doors for me. Telling me it was my time to return home, just as much as hers. A few days into the Holy month of Ramadan I visited Cairo, Egypt. A city of chaos. And a city gifted to carry the resting places of many members of the family of the beloved messenger of Allah, Muhammed ﷺ and where my journey ended.

May Allah open our hearts. May He allow us to always send praise on His beloved messenger ﷺ. May He allow us to always hold his family dear to us. And of those buried in Cairo are, Sayyidi Hussein, Sayyida Nafisa, Sayyida Aisha and Sayyida Zaynab. May He fill us with Baraka. May He fill us with Love. May He fill us with Light. May He gift us with His Presence.

Be

I wish to sing and dance in praise
In praise of Ahmed, Taha, al-Mahy
Envelop me
And bring me to the ocean where I shall sail
On a boat
On wood and waves
And navigate the stars to find my beloved
I gaze at them in awe
The dark night sky, with his light
Reflecting the worlds
Gems floating in the spaces of the universe
Filling it with joy
And I surrender to them
To the light of the worlds
The one who was chosen to give us life

As I am

I am, as I am
Content, peaceful, grateful
These drums play in my chest
And I feel her

She is wonderful, she is blissful, she is sacred
As the olive tree
As the fruits mentioned in holy scripture
As the date from the date tree

She feeds me
Energy
Wholesome and vibrant
Vibrating, I sway, I sway
To the rhythm sown in me by the One
Who gave me life from His breath
I let His rhythm carry me across the seas,
Across the oceans
Endless rivers, lakes and streams
The waters of the cosmos

I am the ocean of the universe
And I swim within her
And I play with her
She pushes her love against me and
Playfully I jump into her
Laughing and embracing one another

indeed the Divine has blessed me
I am wonderful
I am sacred
I am holy
I am beginning as the one He knew I could be
I lay on the ocean buoyant and
Let its waves carry me
In His care, I am at peace

Connected

You are
Connected
Lineage from mountains
Its peaks, its valleys, home of clay
You are
My connection
To the earth I am made from
A part of me
Deeper than I could understand
You are connected
And when you leave
The earth that kept you
Will set you free
And return your soul
To the one whom with
She was meant to be

Traveller

Don't be afraid
Our purpose is
To know
To surrender
To be free
We were made to pass by as travellers

To the Knowers

Take your knowledge
Take the truth
When you go
When you leave to the land hidden in plain sight
Have a peaceful passing
And let go
Take your secrets and watch us from
A close distance
Where you will be free to run across fields
To climb mountains as you once did
The mountains, the heavens and the earth
Watch them
Run. Run free, barefoot.
Sing, laugh, dance
Because your mountains made themselves
A place in heaven
Where Mercy greets you at the gate

A moment

As you hold her
You worry for her
About things once done
Hurtful moments you share

As you hold her
Sing
Sing in remembrance so that she may be
Soothed
So the words of your love, your praise
The truth
Will calm her
And make her feel at ease

Replace the worries
Replace the fears
With those loving lullabies
That make hearts tremble
Remind her
Of the One she loves
Of the One waiting for her

Be the gateway
For her soul to pass in peace

Gateway

My connection
My gate to a world I know not much about
A world forgotten by mankind
Left to crumble after invaders had
Done their job

I think of you
Your life
You went through so much
Subhanallah

I wasn't the closest to you,
But perhaps this was a good thing
So I can remember you in this way
As my chain of authority
To the blood I hold in me

I will go back
I will search the village and beyond
For the traces of me who Know
And find my beloved in every corner of land

When I'm older

I have seen those older than me
Who smile when challenges face them
Who laugh when it doesn't go their way
And who pray
Always pray
Because life is a test and a means to Allah

I have seen those that see Allah in all things
And praise Him with all things

And I have seen those who do not
The complainers
Who see tests as a punishment
And say, "why me, why me?"

I think of myself
I think about the days I'll be old,
Older
I think of the person I wish to be

And I realise

If you want to be like those who see
All as a means
To stay close
Then work now
Force yourself to respond in the best of ways
Soon, it will become your natural way.

Heavy load

You aren't perfect
You live in this world, carrying its weight on
Your shoulders

You bend down to take rest,
Hoping it will lighten the load
That some may decide to carry themselves

Little do you realise whose shoulders you ride on

Shade

Isn't he merciful
Giving way for you to return on a Friday
The day of forgiveness

Isn't he merciful
That people make prayers for your path to be
Cleared of thorns
For you to enter His gardens with peace
With forgiveness
With plants of neverending heights
Reaching eternal heavens
All to give you shade

Nur

I yearn for it
To pray beside others
And listen to the wonders of His words

Ya Allah,
Fill me with Nur
Fill me with life.

A treasured light

His words fill my heart
I listen and hear lights speak
When she glows in love

Her name

Your name comes from great soldiers
An ancient kingdom
Lesser known,
But spread far into mountains

We honour our names
We put them on a pedestal with other things
Hoping it will mean something
Hoping it will make something
And bring a distant memory
Back
With a good name

Little

Do you remember
The past
Sins you committed

Did you ask for forgiveness?
Of the little girl
You once saw

Bloom

She is fierce
Young girl blooming
A strong hand
Soft on the eyes
Even she knows not of the
Fire inside
As of the women whose blood she carries

Ramadan

The month is here
Like a calm breeze that enters
Cooling the eyes of sorrow

Bring me near
And hold me tight
Comfort me and send Your guardians
So that I may receive revelation as it was given

Hussein

I yearn for you
To make visit to the soil you rest on
But I am turned away
By men who know not my reality

The reality of women
Presence so Holy
It was given life by the One
Who cherishes us
Who raises us
Who loves us eternally

And these men
They know not who they turn away
They do not follow what was given to them
They turn a lover away from her beloved

Your grandfather cried
Your beloved grandfather cried
The messenger of Allah cried
For the women who would be turned away from
Their beloved

Muhammed ﷺ

See him
See him in the footsteps you take
Right before left
See him when you smile at others
Wide, from ear to ear
When you greet another, assalamu alaikum

See him
In the revelation you read
Sacred words falling from the tongue of a seeker
Droplets of the purest of water
From the skies that break
In tears
In love

See him
In the one you love
Muhammadan
Written on his forehead
So luminous the stars burst in his sight

See him where others cannot
Where you were gifted to see him

So see him
See him in everything
For everything came from his light

Moments

When I'm with you
The world outside slows down
For a moment time isn't real
It stops so that we may have more of it
And holds us afloat in its stars

Between you and I are the galaxies
Between you and I, there is no separation

And they send their praise
So we may know of their love

Ya Wadud

He sings to me
Words of praise and comfort
To heal an open wound

How did Allah bless me?
Gifted me His most loving
As my guardian
Who cares for me
And loves me in the best of ways

Ya Allah, Ya Allah
Ya Wadud, Ya Wadud
When with him, I am near You

Prayer of a droplet

Ya Allah
Bring me nearer
Make me of the close ones
Of those You love
Those whose every action is a prayer
A drop in an ocean of praise
Let me be of those whom You love
Those whom You fill with Your light
An emblem of the light that You are
A wave in Your vast ocean
Endless

May Allah accept. May Allah put Baraka.

Ameen.

www.ingramcontent.com/pod-product-compliance
Lightning Source LLC
Chambersburg PA
CBHW061322140726
47998CB00007B/2509